LET

God

WRITE YOUR STORY

Dedication

I dedicate this book to the precious girls at **Bridge of Hope Girls' School** in Liberia whose daily transformation l seek and to all girls in other cultures who have been disadvantaged and have suffered as a result of negative culture assumptions.

I also dedicate this book to the late Hero of BOH **Deacon Stephen K. Beyan** who love and passion for girls' education helped me pen this book.

This book is dedicated to my deceased sister **Nancy Dugbor-nyon Weah Tendee.**

Lastly to my wife **Victoria Gbeh Weah**, and our three precious daughter girls **Patience, Pauline & Peace.**

LET

God

WRITE YOUR STORY

———

Copyright ©2023 / Jackson G. Weah
All Rights Reserved

———

ISBN: 979-8-9888993-2-7 - *softcover*
ISBN: 979-8-9888993-3-4 - *ebook*

———

Photography
Tim B. Gilman

Book Design & Production
timmyroland.com

LET

God

WRITE YOUR STORY

Bishop Dr.
Jackson G. Weah

Bridge of Hope
LIBERIA

LET

God

WRITE YOUR STORY

Contents

LET

God

WRITE YOUR STORY

Foreword

Let me begin this foreword with a heart of gratitude and appreciation to Bishop Jackson Weah for asking me to foreword his book. I find this distinctly honoring for a man who was once my professor in Bible College and mentor to revert to me for a foreword for an important project such as this.

I have known Bishop Jackson Weah for nearly 25 years now since my days at the Liberia Christian College in the late 90s and early 2000s and I have known him to be a unique lecturer with a profound passion that goes beyond the classroom imparting the ministries of many ministers young and old he has encountered over the years with humility.

This book addresses a critical and fundamental societal issue that has affected our global village most especially the African continent yea my own country Liberia and that is the problem of the girl child. I am not surprised at all that Bishop Weah has come from a solution oriented direction on this matter because of his passion and the immense energy he has invested in elevating the girl child over the years.

His perspective on this matter without a shadow of doubt brings a whole lot to the table.

Having gone through the pages of this book, I highly recommend it to all who believe in the positive change of our society which begins with elevating the girl child who is the custodian of the very institution on which society is established and that is the family. It is often said "educate a girl child you educate a nation".

Bishop Weah's experience as a little boy in the Weah's village and his passion for the girl child which led to the establishment of the Bridge of Hope a unique school that has positively impacted hundreds of girls over the years puts him in a better position with a great perspective on this subject.

Meanwhile as a proud father of four girls myself and being cognizant of the significance of womanhood in the family, I am highly recommending this book to you who believe in elevating the girl child and changing the narratives that have held the girl child in bondage over the years. Its high time that we all embrace this wave of positive change for the girl child and allow God to write the story for the transformation of lives and the sustenance of hope.

Rev. David Saa Fatorma
Founder & General Overseer
Light Stream Chapel / Solution Outreach Ministries

Foreword

From the early days of knowing Jackson G. Weah, I saw that he was a person with a deep sensitivity and passion for the hurting and dispossessed in society. As we began to work closer together in ministry, I saw this sensitivity and passion, stirred by the Holy Spirit, move him to do things that impacted his congregation and community in transformative ways.

Bridge of Hope Girls School, a tremendous endeavor that has transformed the lives of primary school girls in the Central Matadi community of Liberia, is one of those engagements.

Let God Write Your Story is not simply about primary education, it is about Christ-centered primary education led by Christ-centered people who demonstrate the love of Christ to their students. They also help them engage Christ and their faith in Him in real time, practical ways, while, at the same time, bringing them to the point in the educational process where they allow God to direct and help them prepare for a future that is meaningful, productive, and successful.

This great work will be a catalyst and a tool for others in the Christian educational system, and for Christians in the secular educational system, who want to see real transformation in the lives of their students.

Thank you Bishop Dr. Jackson G. Weah for such an insightful, life-changing work.

Apostle Alfred Jackson
Senior Pastor / Tabernacle of Praise Church International
International Presiding Bishop – TOPAC/KCMI/USA

Foreword

In early 2000 I made my first trip to the continent of Africa. I had accepted an assignment from **PLAN Adoption,** an agency in my hometown, to travel to Liberia and photograph a select group of children that were "eligible" to be adopted by families and given a home here in the US & Canada.

From a very young age I had gazed with awe and wonder at images, stories and film footage of Africa . . . mostly those that the missionaries had brought home as well as having a family subscription to *National Geographic.* I was mesmerized.

When I landed at Roberts Field, just outside of Monrovia, one of the first Liberians that I met was **Jackson Weah** and his lovely wife Victoria. They were a part of a church fellowship that was not only addressing the **spiritual needs** but the **practical** and **survival needs** of their community . . . a community and a nation that had be racked and razed by war, conflict and carnage.

Over the years I have made a total of 3 trips to Liberia and Jackson was always there to do an airport trip . . . run an errand or anything else that needed to be done to make our visit as "smooth" as possible.

In addition Jackson has visited us here in Oregon several times at which time I returned the favor . . . somewhat.

Now here we are almost a quarter of a century later and the *passion, vision* and *pure love of Jesus* that dwells in the Bishop's heart is stronger than ever.

Bridge of Hope is just one of the shining examples of the commitment that he and Victoria have made not only to the girls of Liberia but to the future of the nation . . . their home.

Many Westerners have no clue regarding the history and relationship, sometimes good and sometimes not so good, that the US has in the establishment of Liberia as well as it's future development as an independent nation.

I have learned a lot on this journey. May these pages spark in you the desire to dig in for a deeper understand of our shared history as a nation and in turn our obligation to humanity as a whole.

In this *"Let God Write Your Story"* you will not only get a quick dive into the **History of Liberia** but catch a glimpse of a true **Man of God**.

Tim Gilman
Founder / Creative Director
Museum of Humanity USA

LET

Good

WRITE YOUR STORY

LET *God* WRITE YOUR STORY

Preface

Let God Write Your Story is a captivating story of a 'transformational Christian education model' at Bridge of Hope Girls' School in post war Liberia . . . a model which is transforming the social narratives of disadvantaged girls in the Central New Matadi community and its environs. It is a story of a family with deep passion that muscled courage to bring 're-newed hope' through Christian education to margin-alized teenage girls. *Let God Write Your Story* also unravels deep rooted cultural assumptions faced by a girl-child. She grows up in cultures that don't val-ue her worth and her willingness to aspire to her full potentials like her boy's counterpart. The term "girl-child" as used in this book simply refers to a female offspring under the age of 18. The expression implies that girls are different from boys or face special cir-cumstances.

Let God Write Your Story is also a story of an edu-cation philosophy at Bridge of Hope Girls' School that places intentional emphasis on primary education, which is core to the health of the education system. Liberia's education system at the primary level has been struggling with a faulty foundation. Hence, it is prudent to begin at the very foundation with these vulnerable girls by crafting solid and comprehensive primary education programs considering all major subjects as science, math, language arts, and social studies and with strong emphasis on the reading program for sustainable learning. The words of Johann Amos Comenius reinforced the concept above: "If we want to educate a person on virtue we must polish him [her] at a tender age. If someone is to advance toward wisdom he [she] must be opened up for it is in the first years of his[her] life when his industriousness is still burning , his[her] mind is malleable and his [her] memory still strong." Need to cite the source of this quote.

In a typical Liberian culture there is an age–old negative cultural assumption that "girls/women are another man's property", hence they are in transition and as such they should not be given formal education or have a share in a family's inheritance.

This book is written from a biblical perspective with a clear understanding that a girl-child is equally created in the image of God as her boy counterpart (Gen. 1:26-28). It provides tangible tools and examples that would help transform a girl-child life and sustain her hope.

She is an apex of God's creation and not an extension of her male counterpart. She completes the boy and adds value to his life. She is not an object to be used but a gift to be treasured.

What this book intends to do is to help unfold life complexities, and negative cultural and religious vices that have kept the girl-child and many young women in our cultures in bondage. We may not be able to capture all of the cultural hurdles created overtime in the pathway of a girl-child as she strives to reach her maximum potential, but we are of the strong conviction that the conditions of a girl child expressed in this literature certainly capture the way of life of many girls living in a typical African society.

Each day they struggle with issues such as rejection, abuse. rape lack of acceptance, abandonment, sexual exploitation, very little or no education; lack of role models, etc.. This piece of literature is written to challenge our church and our readers that with these concrete examples and stories of a girl-child, you can muscle courage to transform her roadblocks into resources and bring hope, help and healing to her life.

Our intention in this book is not to engage in the age old controversies that had divided the church over the centuries but rather to add our voice to the many voices crying uncontrollably to transform the social narratives of the girl-child.

We want the national government, parents, community and other stakeholders to pay keen attention to these precious voiceless jewels. We are simply watchmen standing on the walls with a mandate to sound the trumpet for many marginalized teen age girls in rural and urban slums of our nations.

We are calling upon everyone reading this book to join us in this fight against the culture of disparity or unbalanced ratio of boys to education, persistent gender based violence, genital mutilation, boys' preference, rape, illiteracy, poverty etc. that have become the norms of our society.

Let's help the Church and our community understand that 'it is time' to transform the social narratives of the girl-child in our society and that perpetrators of these evil vices against our precious jewels should face the wrath of the law.

Introduction

It was a peaceful afternoon in Wekablee (Weah's village) when the sun was descending with a smile on river *Dan'ton*. I heard the villagers praising the Almighty God *'A'r poo a'r Baa Zlan zuo'* (Krahn dialect), who gives (*Dan'ton*) to water our land and cause our crops to grow. It never goes dry even when rivers in other villages are dried. Life in the village greatly depended on (*Dan'ton*). The rain had gone and the dry season was emerging with a very strong wind blowing across Wekablee (Weah's village). Little kids were half naked playing different games in the village square. Women and young girls were fetching water from the (*Dan'ton*) while others were returning from the farms with bundle of woods and basket of fruits on their heads. Did I see some men freely walking?

Yes, I saw old man Gaye, my grand uncle, with his hands swinging and joyously whispering while his fourth and youngest wife *Boryea* age 17, carried bundle of woods on her head, of course she was pregnant, but also with baby on her back while trying to help two of her mate's children walk along the narrow path that leads back to the village. I was puzzled but this was a normal life style of the village. Men allowed their wives to go through these kinds of rigorous domestic duties while they sat and watched them without helping. This was my world and everything seemed to be in harmony. The community was well governed as my Dad and the elders gave leadership to their fellow kinsmen. Young boys and girls were required to respect the elders and live by the rules that governed the community. The bush schools (poro and sande') had taught them how to honor the elders and respect rules that governed the clan as they transitioned into adulthood. Western education had not spread like in our modern days and only few had access to education, mostly the boys.

My Dad told me how he sent his first son to Sierra Leone to be educated, but the plan was swiftly aborted when he recalled his son for reasons he never disclosed. The elders of our land never dreamt that one day their beautiful ancestral homeland would be devastated by a senseless civil war that could send them back across the *Cestos River*.

Of course history tells us that they had come from across the Cestos as refugees hundreds of years ago during their time of the French Colonial Revolution. As we continued to play in the village square, the songs and sound of drums continued to echo from the direction of a nearby village. As the music grew nearer the melody became so pleasant. We all abandoned our games and without slippers and shirts joyously joined in the parade.

Little did I know that it was leading to my Father's compound for a wedding ceremony actually (dowry payment) of his daughter--my sister. She was like a tender plant shooting up at the end of a rainy season. During the last harvesting season she graduated from the bush school. Did I remember that her graduation lasted for a week?

Boys in our village literally chased after her to take her hand in marriage, but this one young man from the next village succeeded in capturing her attention. Maybe it was because of his status.

The marriage ceremony was successfully conducted as the custom dictates between the two communities; and for nearly two weeks there were elaborate celebrations. She got married at an early age but was not privileged to sit in the classroom even though the husband claimed to have been literate. Twenty years later this well celebrated marriage took a dramatic turn after bearing eleven children for the husband. Her values and dignity as a woman were abused.

She had no formal education and the husband took no interest in educating her. The husband took several concubines. I am yet to understand his ultimate intention. It leaves me to do more research to hopefully capture the inherent ideals behind such a practice in my next book.

My sister was abandoned in the village along with her twelve children while the husband moved to the city with his concubines. We faithfully supported her over the years until her untimely demise in 2008 in a tragic motor accident. It grieved me that my sister would suffer at the hands of a man who claims he was educated (semi- literate man) but did not value girls' education and the sanctity of young women.

Let God Write Your Story captures the tears and untold stories of my sister and many other teenage girls living in the remote villages and urban slums of our nations. As was captured in our doctoral dissertation, systematic violence perpetrated against teenage girls and women throughout the civil war in Liberia.

This left negative impact on the lives of the girl–child. These and many prevailing situations against the girl-child in our nation have created an urgency to make concrete interventions in girls' education. Thank God for the many proactive measures in post war Liberia by many stakeholders.

The words of Nelson Mandela captured the future of Liberian girls:

"A winner is a dreamer who never gives up."

Surely the girls are all winners. They are not only dreaming about the prospect of their lives but many faithful Christians like you and me are translating their dreams into decisions to provide tangible solutions to their plights. Whatever we do as an individual or nation should help to transform their lives and sustain the hope God has placed in these girls.

God is saying to the girls of Liberia I have a good thought towards you. It is a thought of good (high prospect of a future and hope) and not of evil (Jer. 29:10-11).

Let us journey in *'Let God Write Your Story,'* as I have used Bridge of Hope Girls' School as a case study to tell the untold stories of many teenage girls asking God to write their stories. Unless God writes our story it is merely a tale of an epic tragedy without purpose. He is the author of our story, (Hebrews. 12:2) Let God write what He wants to in your story and finish it. Let Him mark up your story the way He

LET

God

WRITE YOUR STORY

Chapter 1

Culture of Disparity

& VICIOUS CIRCLES OF ILLITERACY

Liberia, like many other African countries, finds herself with an unbalanced ratio of girls to boys undergoing education.[1] Levels of education and literacy in Liberia are extremely low for everyone, but substantially worse for females. 41% of women, contrasted with 70% of men, are literate. 56% of females and 39% percent of males have never attended any school. In the northwestern areas of Liberia, 70% of females have no education at all.[2] 25% of females and 26% of males have only a primary education.

And the 29% of urban women who have attended some secondary school contrasts with only 6% of rural women. Urban residents tend to be considerably more educated than their rural counterparts. 70.7% of urban men have secondary education or higher as compared to 45.8% of urban women. The limited availability of schools in rural areas, where most of the indigenous people live, makes the percentage

---

1 - Peter Ben. Deputy Ministry of Education. UNMIL Regular
    Press Briefing. Liberian Government drafts national policy
    on girls education. January 29, 2006.
2 - Compare with DHS p.31: In Northwestern region,

even more staggering with 10.4% for women and 37.4% for men.[3]

The fact is that in most cases, girls and women lag far behind boys and men, educationally.

In my first book, *Rewriting Your Story*, I captured the journey of my sister that led to her death. Both my sister and biological mother never had the opportunity to get a formal education. As I am reminded of this tragic story in my life, I was captivated to provide Christian education for the over two hundred fifty disadvantaged young girls currently at the Bridge of Hope Girls' School.

A part of my goals in this second book is to re-awaken the church and the community to join in the campaign to create more awareness for many teenage girls and young women in my culture that still suffer and live without formal education. Join me in doing so by telling the untold stories of these girls.

As I delve into the lives of the underprivileged girls at Bridge of Hope, it helps to find answers to the many questions that loom in my mind about the plights of a girl-child in my culture. My intention is to unravel, capture, and provide concrete solutions to the numerous unseen tears and traumas of disadvantaged girls in the informal settings and villages of our nations who may not have a chance to be heard and experienced any transformation.

Unless believers like you and me rise up and leave our ego and stand up against the negative cultural and

---

3 - Ibid

religious assumptions meted against them, their lives will never be transformed.   Come with me as we unravel their pains, traumas, tears, and frustrations, and see how God has been transforming trash into treasures at the Bridge of Hope Girls' School. Please join me as we allow God to write their stories. I am certain by reading these starling accounts of these girls you would allow God to write your own story.

Many volumes have been written in recent times on the subject of gender equality as we embrace change in the 21st century. The education of girls and women has been a central concern of the international community for at least three decades. Though much progress have been made since the world conference on education for all, the situation of girls remains deeply worrying in several underdeveloped world countries including Liberia.

Let God Write Your Story is not just another volume but a compelling voice calling on the sleeping Church to rise to the task of God's original design for teenage girls. Let me remind all men reading this book that both men and women have a shared origin, a shared destiny, a shared tragedy, and a shared hope.[4]

In simple words we were all created in the image of God (shared origin), all were given the power to dominate (shared destiny), and we all sinned (shared tragedy), but we were all forgiven in Christ (shared hope). Let us stop this negative theology that women were responsible for the sins that came upon all

---

4 - Loren Cunningham, Hamilton et. Al. Why Not Woman pg. 93.

creatures (Gen. 3:7). We all fell short of the glory of God and received equal forgiveness. May God help us through this book to value teenage girls and young women so as to create a safe space to unlock their intelligence, their passion, and all the great things they hold within themselves.[5]

The Church has paid deaf ears and blind eyes to this important matter. In my mind she has not done enough to alleviate the situation. Some say that the matter of women and girls is the most divisive issue to confront the Church since the Reformation.

Bible-believing people are coming down on opposite sides of this argument, often with more heat than light in their discussion. Others try to ignore it altogether, thinking it is not their battle but a controversy between fringe elements. This issue is hardly one involving a fringe element or a side concern. It's an issue that goes to the very core of the church, the culture, and every nation. When we look at this issue of the role of women and girls, we are entering humanity's most ancient battleground- the war of the serpent against the woman.[6]

Considering the sweeping realities of women equality in the corporate world, the Church should rise up to the uncompromising task at hand. The Church is slow to adapt this change due to religious, traditional and cultural practices; hence the church is struck in the past. As I think of the behaviors of the Church towards teenage girls and women's edu-

---

5 - Leymah Gbowee, Nobel Peace Laureate and President of GPFA.
6 - Loren Cunningham, Hamilton et al. Why Not Woman. P. 55

cation, this Russian proverb helped to described their actions: "He who live in the past loses an eye." May God help the emerging church leaders of this century to embrace change regarding this matter and yet remain faithful to the authority of scripture.

In the language of the curse, the man *"shall rule over you"* (Genesis 3:16). We must never forget that the domination of women by men that fills our history books and our cultures is not a part of God's good creation but as a result of the fall, hence the tension, the conflict, hierarchy. As David Hubbard has noted, since the fall "human life has been vacillating between the grasping femininity which competes with man and man's blind dominion over woman which degrades personality and destroys partnership." [7]

Let God Write Your Story does not intend to engage humanity's most ancient battleground concerning this issue of women and young girls, rather we've come to encourage one another in truth, allowing the Holy Spirit's healing to transform us. Our motivation is predicated on the fact that many innocent teenage girls and young women are languishing in slums and villages of our post war Liberia whose images have been daunting due to discrimination and prejudice, wrong traditional, cultural and religious assumptions. It is obvious to my reader that a girl is twice as likely not to be educated as a boy in any culture.

This book captures the stories, tears and traumas of teenaged girls and young women in a nation torn and devastated by civil strife for fourteen years. It is a

---

7 - David Hubbard. Why Not Woman. P. 55

story of an education model that brings transformation to a girl child who seeks to reclaim her lost image and identity in a man dominated society. Let God Write Your Story seeks to go deeper to unravel strong and negative cultural assumptions that attempt to exclude teenage girls from excelling and realizing their full potentials.

In the words of Madam Leymah Gbowee, Nobel Peace Laureate;

> *"All girls are asking us to do is create that space to unlock the intelligence, unlock the passion, unlock all of the great things that they hold within themselves".*[8]

Let God Write Your Story shares the story of a journey of a girl child from exclusion to embrace. We attempt, with deep passion, to capture the many wounds and pains inflicted on an innocent girl child in a male-dominated culture that keep suppressing her desire to reach her full potential.

This book attempts to tell the story of over two million vulnerable girls mostly in South Saharan Africa with a huge percentage in my war torn nation (Liberia) that are mutilated through female circumcision to diminish their sexual desire. Little girls who survive the procedure grow up to face painful sex, possible infertility, and a greater chance of dying during childbirth.[9]

---

8 - Leymah Gbowee, Nobel Peace Prize Laureate and President of GPFA.
9 - Story compiled thanks to Abraham Conneh, Education
   Programme Officer, Oxfam GB Liberia and Heather Johnston,
   West Africa Regional Education Programme Manager, Oxfam GB.

I encourage my reader to journey along with me as we chronicle the story of rape, rejection, child labor, prostitution, and low self esteem of a girl child in post war Liberia. Let's allow God to write the story of their loss of identities as they embrace change in the digital age and loss of vital cultural heritage of their villages and towns. Let us allow God to write the story.

I am asking my reader to journey with me as I narrate the plights of teenage girls before and after the civil war conflict in Liberia. Teenage girls already had fewer educational opportunities than boys, kept out of school by discrimination, poverty and household obligations and boys' preference. With the eruption of the civil war in December 1989, inequality in education was exacerbated.

Thousands of girls were the targets of specific physical and emotional gender based violence and abuse such as rape, forced prostitution, torture, forced termination of pregnancies and mutilation. Statistics show that between 2000 and 2002 girls' gross enrollment ratio declined from 72.5% to 35.5%. In an effort to address the gender disparities and high level of gender violence against girls, the Liberian Ministry of Education worked with UNICEF to develop a national policy on girls' education.[10] This noble initiative could not achieve its intended goal as the national government had failed to make budgetary allocations for the Girl's Unit at the Ministry of Education.

---

10 - Story compiled thanks to Abraham Conneh, Education
Programme Officer, Oxfam GB Liberia and Heather Johnston,
West Africa Regional Education Programme Manager, Oxfam GB.

Let God Write Your Story is a voice for the many girls that have been excluded from, kept out of school or those who never made it to schools, because of gender, ethnicity, age, poverty and socio-economic status, linguistic background, place of residence, disability or any other reason. The girls are our primary concern and I say let God transform their stories. I am convinced that the Church of Jesus Christ should play a proactive role in championing the cause of this most vulnerable constituency. The Church is a major stakeholder hence they must work hard to promote the basic ideals of Christ's Kingdom in regards to the liberation of girls and women.

Let it be known here that when Christians perpetuate bias against women and young girls, the message it sends is that God is unjust. Christian leaders acting unjustly, reflects on the character of God who loves and accepts every gender. Christianity, the vehicle for propagating the ideals of Christ and his kingdom, should offer women equality as well and set the stage to discover God's purposes for the Church and His Kingdom here on earth as it relates to the different genders. Unfortunately, the Church ,at times, has not accurately reflected that truth.

In the beginning God made both man and woman in his image (*imago dei*). Neither man nor woman is made more in the image of God than the other. From the beginning the Bible places both man and woman at the pinnacle of God's creation. Neither sex is exalted and neither depreciated. Being created in the image of God simply means to relate in a holy and perfect way to each other. Of course, different people play different roles, giving them different levels of authority at certain times. But those roles are not based solely on gender or race or some other physical characteristics. They are based on gifting, calling, and need.[11]

This book is a result of my doctoral dissertation during my nearly six year's journey at the Africa International University in Nairobi Kenya. Most of what is written in this book are the findings from my research and my long experience of working with girls at the Bridge of Hope Girls' School in Liberia, the school my wife and I founded after my graduate studies at Nairobi Evangelical Graduate School of Theology (NEGST; now Africa International University).

---

11 - Women in Leadership, vCCol. 3.3. pg. 40

LET

God

WRITE YOUR STORY

Chapter 2

Original Design

FOR A GIRL CHILD

In Jeremiah 29:10 -11 . . .

This is what the Lord says: "When seventy years are completed for Babylon, I will come to you and fulfill my gracious promise to bring you back to this place. For I know the plans I have for you declares the Lord, plans to prosper you and not harm you, plans to give you hope and a future.

I have read this passage several times and considered its immediate context; how it speaks to the Jews in Babylonian captivity. Covenant keeping God remembers his promises made to his chosen people concerning their possible return to the Promised Land after seventy years in captivity. God spoke "I know the plans towards you, it is a plan of good and not of evil, to give a future and hope."

I am certain this portion of Scripture is applicable in the context of girls and women in our society that are disadvantaged because of negative cultural, traditional and religious assumptions in our society. Like the Jews in Babylonia, women and teenage girls the world over ,especially south of the Sahara, have been exiled by negative cultural, traditional and religious assumptions for many centuries. Women have been kept in bondage, crying and calling for their liberations.

This is the genesis of many women's movements in our society today. God is speaking to the church in this generation and, most especially in Liberia, that the exilic period of women and teenage girls is over and He is returning them to the original design before the fall. Jesus came to set in motion the healing God had promised when Adam and Eve shared the great tragedy of the garden. He came to end the painful consequences of a broken and sinful world, including the rift between men and women. Jesus came to set men and women free, but because of the terrible exclusion that women had suffered, His open welcome meant even more to them.[12]

Women have been offered so little in a hostile world. In the words of one author, "Jesus did not start a movement for women, but a movement for humans. It is not surprising, however, that women were especially responsive to his ideas. Trapped in the isolation of a sometimes hostile family, civil war, disease, poverty, abused, rejection, women knew how insecure, unjust and lonely the world was."[13] Let it be clear here that Jesus' mission wasn't gender biased; it was gender inclusive. Jesus said, "All that the Father gives me will come to me, and whoever comes to me I will never drive away." (John 6:37)

---

12 - Loren Cunningham, Hamilton et al. Why Not Woman. Pg. 111-112..
13 - Elise Boulding, the Underside of History: A View of Women
       Through Time (Boulder: Westview Press, 1976), 358.

He did not come to bring about a women's revolution but liberation to these precious people. Let it be known that they were created in the same image as men and they help to complete men. In the words of Faustin Ntamshobora Transformation Through The Other: "Women seek to complement men in that we are incomplete without the other."[14] Truly women complete men, as they are a gift and special companion to us.

God's original intention for creating women was not for men to rule or have dominion over them as been propagated by religions, cultures and traditions. Women were not to be considered as second class citizens or domestic animals as has been communicated over the centuries. When God created man and woman neither sex was exalted to be a dominant sex to rule and have dominion over the other, rather both of them were created equal and given the mandate to rule the earth and not over each other. Prior to the fall here what was said about the woman:

So God created man in his own image, in the image of God created him, male and female created *them*. And God blessed *them*, and God said to *them*,

"Be fruitful, and increase in number, fill the earth and subdue it. Rule over the fish of the sea, and over the birds of the air, and over every living thing that moves on the ground. Gen. 1:27-28.

---

14 - Faustin Dissertation

And the Lord God said it is not good that the man should be alone . . .

I will make him a helper suitable for him
Gen. 2:18.

The phrase *"Man shall rule over you or your desire shall be to your husband"* came after the fall.

> *And I will put enmity between thee and the woman and between thy seed and her seed: It shall bruise thy heed and thou shall bruise his heel. Unto the woman he said I will greatly multiply thy sorrow and thy conception: In sorrow thou shall bring forth children and thy desire shall be to thy husband and he shall rule over you. Gen.3:15-16.*

The phrase was not a mandate but a message, which was given as a result of the mess caused by Adam and Eve. The message is directly set in the context of hope announced in Gen. 3:15 of the coming of the Seed of a woman (Jesus) who was going to crush the head of Satan through his redemptive work on Calvary. Traditionally, we have been taught to believe that it was the woman who bears the greater weight of the sin of probation in the Garden of Eden.

It is an age-old fallacy and incorrect interpretations coupled with bias theological assumptions we all have carried too long. It is time to say enough is enough! The both of them shared equal responsibility of the fall in the garden and no one is more guilty or responsible than others.

God's original plan seeks to dispel all negative cultural assumptions against a woman or girl child in every culture including war ravaged Liberia. Every girl child battles with the fact that she has been thought of as a second-class or domestic slave to be ruled by her male counterpart. She wrestles with the fact that cultural and traditional hierarchy led by man has marred her identity. She seeks to find her place of prominence, yet she is held captive by background noise that hinders her progress to excel. She is seeking help but from the wrong source (male counterparts). I speak to that little girl today that you are in the process of time and the Potter who knows your hurts is shaping and remolding your life.

It might seem like an impossible and fruitless battle, but I am saying "impossible itself says I am possible." You will certainly make it; there is still hope! God is in His destiny storeroom designing your destiny and when he is done you will be the vessel of honor fit for the master's use. I challenge you today not to" trade pride for popularity."

This book seeks to share the story of how a girl child is pointed back to her Creator whose original intention is to ensure that she equally prospers, and has hope and a future like the boy child. The culture has favored the boy over you but God doesn't and so there is still hope.

God's original intent for a girl child is to ensure her that she was created in His image with all the qualities and abilities like her male counterpart. She was created to co-rule with his male counterpart and have dominion over every living thing that moves upon the earth. Let God write your story is simply an example of hope intended to help raise the low self esteem of a girl child who is desperately seeking a meaning in life. She is in the middle of a vast world seeking for a role model but searching in all the wrong places.

Listen, her frustrations have led her to go after the fleeting culture of this generation that prides itself in consumerism, electrical gadgets, drugs, alcohol, pornography, and sex. She must be rescued through the authority of Scripture and not lean on the negative cultural assumptions of our society that says that she is nothing but a domestic slave to men.

When God writes your story He does so by shaping your lives to bring you to the place of rich fulfillment in your life even as a girl child. This is the way He helps to shape the destiny of your life in the midst of life's devastations and despairs. God is seeking to bring revelations out of devastations in the life of that one little girl in the remote village of Liberia, slum of Kibera, war torn DRC, Sierra Leone, and Rwanda, who is bitterly crying after her mother and father had been killed as a result of senseless civil wars initiated and perpetuated by our greedy African politicians.

Let God write your story by permitting him to mold, shape, and reshape your life to his original intent for you. You were created to rule and have dominion and not to be ruled! Allow yourself to rest in His presence with great patience and hope in the midst of life's dangers and allow Him to fully direct your path (Prov. 3: 5-6). Let Him cultivate the hope that builds and anchors in the sure foundation. Above all allow God to direct your life one day at a time and give him the chance to work in, through and with you so as to bring you to place of hope. In this way you will be recognizing the hands of God upon your life as it unfolds steadily in the midst of despairs and discouragements; knowing that his presence brings you hopes and gives you a new name.

Let God write your story is a story of God's unconditional love in spite of our failures and faults. What happens when God writes your story? He creates a new identity for you. Yes! He turns your trash into treasures and your dirt into dignity.

LET

God

WRITE YOUR STORY

Chapter 3

Capturing the Tears

AND TRAUMAS A GIRL CHILD

In *Let God Write Your Story* we consciously remind a girl-child that, in the words of Jocelyn Soriano: "To be rejected by someone doesn't mean you should also reject yourself or that you should think of yourself as a lesser person. It doesn't mean that nobody will ever love you anymore. Remember that only ONE person has rejected you at the moment, and it only hurts so much because to you, that person's opinion symbolized the opinion of the whole world, of God." [15]

God is at work in your story and writing each page of your life that no man can alter. It is a book that no man can delete what has been written. He knows the details of your life even before you were conceived in your mother's womb.

The loving Father knows your fears and frustrations, your heights and lows. He knows what is around the next curve. He is the speed breaker on your highway and takes care of the potholes along your path. For you to be able to let God write your new story, you must move on from your previous

---

15 - Jocelyn Soriano, Mend My Broken Heart

chapter and turn the pages to start a new chapter in your life.[16]

Allow Him to write your story. Each of us has a story. Commit yours to the Lord and allow him to intervene and give it a new meaning. It is important to know who you truly are. Who you are not what others say about you or even what you think or how you feel about yourself.

Others may have called you a stupid or hopeless girl. Your mates may say you are weird and your teacher concludes you are a mistake or failure. You may have been told again and again that you will not make it in life. The sad thing is, you feel stupid and have come to think they all must be right. What I want you to realize is that what they say, or what you feel or think does not matter; what matters is to remember what God says about you in his Word.

I am a child of God (John 1:12), I am the light of the world –Mtt.5:14, I am an ambassador of Christ –(2 Cor.5:10), I am Christ's friend (Jn.15:15), I am God's dwelling place his temple (I Cor.6:19), I am joint heirs with Christ- I share his inheritance (Rom. 8:17).

You may be living with a stigma of rape, HIV and AIDS, domestic violence, poverty, emotional tortures, resentments, and even the scourge of civil wars. Allow God to handle all of these life complexities. When God writes your story he transforms your story into glory. I pray also that the eyes of your heart

---

16 - Milton Kelly - Let God guide the pen when you write your story, July 23, 2003

be enlightened in order that you may know the hope to which he has called (Eph.1:17).

The term "girl-child" implies that girls are different from boys or face special circumstances.[17] All children are created with dignity including the girl-child. In many cultures including Liberia, girls are seen as having problems but it is equally true that they have potential.

Every child has a problem as well as potential and we should endeavor to work on transforming their problems into potentials. In my culture girls are seen as a man's property and are never intended to stay home and bear the family's name. They are considered as always being in transition. Hence they are not fully included as part of the family and should not be educated or given an inheritance. Girls are often neglected, exploited, abused and discriminated against. Capturing the words of David Kupp when he said "

"Girls are not usually visible on statistical profiles. Their predicament is blended with those of women or boys." [18]

In Let God write your story we are convinced that a girls access to education and legal rights can break the cycle of poverty and discrimination that girls face around the world.

---

17 - Desiree Segura-April. The Girl – Child and Positive Youth Development. Asbury Seminary. CD 551 Children's Seminar. March 19, 2011.
18 - David Kupp .Development Education Manager for World Vision Canada (1994, 2).

Here are some common
sayings of girls in some cultures.

"Girls are maggots in the rice"
(an old Chinese saying)

"Daughters and dead fish are no keeping wares."
(an English saying from the 18th century).

"Daughters are water spilled on the ground."
(Taiwan)

"A daughter is 'only a prostitute' who will be
exchanged for cattle at the time of marriage."
(among the Iteso in Uganda)

A girl is "merely a weed."
(Among Zulus)

"Happy is he whose children are sons
and woe to him whose children are daughters."
(From Talmudic writings).

"A girl lets you down twice, once at birth
and the second time when she marries."
(A Korean saying)

Announcement of the birth
of a female child: "Nothing was born."
(Among Hindus).

"A girl – child is another man's property,
she was never intended to stay at home."
(A Liberian saying)

Let God write your story is praying for transformation in a typical Liberian culture wherein these
negative cultural assumptions can be overturned because "It takes only one word to hurt a girl-child, a

matter of seconds, and one stupid, impatient blow of the crop. But winning back her trust takes years. And sometimes there isn't the time."[19]

One wise decision a girl-child must make is to accept and appreciate herself the way God made her. "When you stop living your life based on what others think of you real life begins. At that moment, you will finally see the door of self-acceptance opened." [20]

The truth is that none of us are perfect—each one has one flaw or another. There is nothing you can do about your genes, which you inherited from your parents. They affect the shape of your nose, legs, eyes, height, color, etc. If there is something you can do about a weak area, go ahead and do it. For example, if you have bad breath, brush your teeth after each meal and chew a minty gum; it will help you freshen your breath. If you have an offensive body odor, bathe twice daily, use a body spray or a sweet smelling talcum powder or rub lemon under your armpit.

If you are overweight then cut down on junk food, eat natural foods like fruits and vegetables. Exercise more and replace juices (artificial) with natural God–given water. Self-acceptance does not mean you deny what you don't like ,but you choose to say or think *"I wish my legs were longer but since God chose to make me this way it means that is the way he wants me to look for a purpose."* His word says, "I am fearfully and wonderfully made." (Ps. 139:14) That must be true because God cannot lie. I am beau-

---

19 - Nina George, The Little Paris Bookshop
20 - http://sumo.ly/as0A via @sepi_tajima

tiful and not another man's property or a weed. Self acceptance produces peace and joy within you plus it boosts your self–confidence. Marilyn Monroe drove home the concept of self-acceptance when she asserted "wanting to be someone else is a waste of the person you are."[21] In this book , we define self-acceptance as "living the life you choose to live without worrying what others think about you." It doesn't matter what someone else thinks about you." What matters is what you think about yourself (in line with the Word of God). I say to that one girl reading this book you are more of a super model than a girl on the cover page of any magazine.

Trauma and tears of Boryea[22]

It was Monday morning when I walked to the first grade class at the Bridge of Hope Girls' School and saw little girls ages 6-8 comfortably seated on armed chairs, in a modern well ventilated building, happy and learning. I reflected on my niece Boryea who started school with me in the village. Our school was built out of dirt bricks and had one single classroom and teacher. We sat on dirt floors or little chairs brought from our homes. Boryea was a young beautiful girl with a great future. She was fortunate because my Uncle allowed her among his daughters, to attend school. Most of her other siblings were given in to early marriages after the initial rite of passage. Girls were not encouraged to go to school in my village. Rather, they were given in early,

---

21 - Marilyn Monroe, http://sumo.ly/as0A via @sepi_tajima
22 - This is not her name; since she is still alive we don't anyone
        to stigmatize and humiliate her for allowing us to share her story.

forced or pre-arranged marriages. In this story I want to capture the tears, pains and traumas of Boryea and how her dream for a brighter future was shattered. Like Boryea many girls are still languishing in the slums and villages of our nation who need just a word "hope." *Let God Write Your Story* is about sharing hope, help and healing with that one girl or young woman feeling discriminated against in our society.

We walked three hours daily to and from school and had great fun on our way back home. We had to cross the Youkor river and at times we stopped at the stream to take a fresh bath after a long walk under the scourging sun. Our school was not like Bridge of Hope Girls' School where students are seated in armed chairs, good floors, glass windows, and good ventilation. Our teachers never had the opportunity like BOH teachers to have desks in the classroom. We did not have indoor toilets, offices, and a big chapel for devotions. We had our devotion on an open field and, we hoisted up the Liberian flag while we sang the National Anthem.

The ENI Mission School (Elizabeth National Institute) ,owned and operated by the Association of Independent Churches of Africa, headed by the late Bishop Augustus B. Marwieh, was the only Christian school in our village. The school started with one teacher and later it was increased to three. Our school was housed in one big classroom with no partition, so students were seated in different corners of the room. We had no floors and the walls were not cemented or painted. Did I remember that we had no blackboard and sometimes no chalk? Yes!

The teachers use dried cassava and we mostly learned by rote memory reciting the alphabet very loudly. Most of the childrens' toes were infested with jiggers (a tiny insect that infested the toes of most children in African villages). I remembered it was from kindergarten to 3rd grade. It was fun being in school for the first time. I was so excited because of the new experience. I was just eleven. We spoke pageant English but this was just while we were in class and at home we spoke our local dialects.

Boryea, age 12, was very regular and we made it to school every morning with other children from the nearby villages. We dressed in blue and white uniforms with no slippers. My dad would dress me with my shirt tucked in my short trousers each morning before reaching the school.

Do I remember my dad giving us lunch? No! But he made sure we had enough rice and soup (mostly palm butter) in the morning before going to class.

All of our teachers were male and the majority of the students were boys. Most of the parents did not send their girls to school for fear that when educated, they would abandon the traditional ways of their clan. Many of the girls were over-aged and also felt ashamed to be in school, so they chose to stay at home and do normal household chores and later got married to boys who had no formal education, thus bearing children who were just as illiterate as their parents. The circle of illiteracy and poverty continues in my village, producing so many children who were social liabilities to the community. This was the culture I grew in and little did I know that one day I would help to bring about transformation more so for the girls who may want to follow the ways of their parents. My childhood experiences led me to engage in creating a new identity for Liberian girls at the Bridge of Hope Girls' School after many years.

Boryea and I made it to school for two years until the third year when she started escaping days in school. I wonder what was going on with my niece. One day we were walking from school and Boryea was so weak and could not walk. I literally helped her to cross the bridge and reach the village. Boryea became so sick and after a few weeks that the news about Boryea's pregnancy spread in the village like a wildfire. It was a tight secret among the mothers but young people whispered it among themselves until it reached the ears of our dad.

He was a strong man who believed in principles, so he challenged the issue thus reaching to the bottom. A well-respected man who was an elder of the clan and leader in the AICA Church in our village could not sit idle to see such an abuse go unpunished. Dad was my mentor and my hero. He summoned the mothers and then make inquiry into Boryea's pregnancy. At that meeting fear gripped everyone. My dad was ready to react to this unfortunate situation by descending on the perpetrator.

The story was sad as more revelations surfaced about my niece's pregnancy. When my dad finally learned that it was one of the village teachers who had impregnated innocent Boryea, the entire village was inflamed. She was indeed innocent and striving to keep her virginity, but was abused by the village teacher who did not live up to his professional ethics. My dad, being the School Board Chairman, vehemently confronted the teacher in question and he was dismissed and driven from the village.

Boryea lived with the stigma and shame and could not associate nor move around the village. My parents kept her on the farm. Many days Boryea cried when her friends came to visit with her after school. One day I went to visit her after school and asked her how she was feeling now that she was not in school. Boryea said, "I know our Dad will not allow me to go back to school. That means my hope for the future is shattered." I will not know how to read and write and even speak better English. I can't go to the city and find a good job and help our parents.

Tell me uncle. I feel so ashamed and I don't know how it all happened. You know he deceived me by saying he would marry me, take me to the city and send me to school. I resisted for a long time, but he kept pursuing me until it happened. I lost my virginity to a man who had lied to me. Boryea sat in tears and,embracing her, we wept together. I said to myself, "Why did she not report this incident in the early stage when this unprofessional teacher made these unwholesome advances at her?"

This is what we teach girls at Bridge of Hope to do when men make sexual advances at them and try to lure them into sexual behaviors. We tell them to sound the alarm even if it was their own relations. In a culture where older men molest young girls, we must teach our girls to resist as well as condemn such unwholesome behaviors in the strongest terms.   We also work along with the girls in our counseling program at BOH to help them understand that they can remember the hurt, the injustice, and the trauma, but they must learn to forgive the sinner."[23]

Rape is very common in my culture, but most of time, the case is swept under the carpet or compromised among relatives. Girls who left the village for the city to live with extended families to get an education normally experience these unwholesome practices from their close families such as uncles, nephews, grandpa, or stepfather.

These were days in Liberia when we had no human rights advocates to speak about rape and sexual abuse. These vices go unpunished because we live in a close and compromising society.   Boryea was sexually exploited and actually raped because she was under age. The Liberian culture is a culture of shame and honor. In such a culture issues of rape and sexual exploitations would be kept as a family's secret for the fear of stigma and public ridicule. It has to stop and we are encouraging parents to report cases of rape in their community so as to prevent evil men from abusing our innocent young girls.

Truly Boryea read the mind of our dad who decided from this point on not to educate any of his girls-child for the fear of being abused by the teachers. Thirty five later, Boryea is old and uneducated

---

23 - Cathy Burnham Martin, The Bimbo Has Brains:
    And Other Freaky Facts

with five children from different fathers, living in a cycle of illiteracy and poverty in our village. Three of her girls are still in refugee camps in Guinea, married to uneducated men because Boryea had a negative experience in school. This story is a reminder that uneducated mothers most often do not encourage their girls to be educated. Hence,there is a vicious cycle of illiteracy and poverty in the family, more so among the girls.

In the words of
Ban Ki Moon, UN Secretary General

> *"Investing in girls and women is likely to prevent inter-generational cycles of poverty and yield high economic and societal returns."*[24]

That is our motivation--to educate girls in Liberia because with this, everything changes. She will be three times less likely to get HIV/AIDs, earn twenty percent more income and have a smaller, healthier family. There is a saying in Central Africa that "Education opens the girl's eyes."[25]

We are waging war on illiteracy and engaging in this rescue mission because illiteracy is a powerful shackle for those who would like to keep others in submission. Liberia has to deal with this monster or else we may return to the dark days of our nation's past when illiterate young boys and girls were drugged and forced to take up arms to kill their own people

---

24 - Ban Ki Moon cite correct reference
25 - Source: Learning: *The Treasure Within*. Report to UNESCO of the International Commission on Education for the Twenty-first Century. Paris, UNESCO, 1996.

during our fourteen years of senseless civil war. It still puzzles me in a nation where 85% of the population is illiterate with 90% among girls and women; and yet, some men in high governmental positions or decision makers who, in all good faith, question the necessity of educating a girl-child or make ironic remarks about female education.

> "A respect for equity demands a special effort to do away with all inequality between the sexes in the field of education. Gender inequality lies at the root of the lasting situations of inferiority that affect women at every stage of their lives. Yet, the strategic importance of women's education for development is today acknowledged by all experts. A very clear correlation has been established between the educational level of women and the overall improvement in the population's health and nutrition and the drop in fertility rates."[26]

The benefits of educating girls and women can therefore never be over-stressed. The first person to benefit from education is the woman or girl herself, as an individual and as a member of society. However, the positive effects are also felt by her family, the community, society and the whole country. You will not only support your families, but also influence policies and help communities in a powerful way.

---

26 - Source: Learning: *The Treasure Within.* Report to UNESCO of the International Commission on Education for the Twenty-first Century. Paris, UNESCO, 1996

Young girls and women let God write your story and take you from despair to destiny. If you allow him, you could move beyond just mere secondary schools to colleges and universities where more doors of work opportunities would be open to you. "All women are powerful; some just need help realizing the power within them."[27]

We at Bridge of Hope Girls' School aim to bring a new identity to an underprivileged girl child living in post conflict Liberia who may get married as young as 13 if she is not rescued.

Captivating stories from girls

" . . . By the age of eight my mom began
to sell me to a man in exchange for money."

This captivating story is from a girl in the Central Matadi (actual name withheld) but for the sake of identity we called her Lebeh. She told us how she had wanted to share her story for a long time, but something held her back. Lebeh lived in the slum Matadi community in an unfinished building. She narrated her own story: "It all started when I was eight years old and was sexually assaulted by my most admirable uncle. I have tried to keep this thing off my memory but it keeps bouncing back to me." She asserted, "It is time to share my story so that many other girls can be helped in the process."

"I was raised single handedly by my mother and never knew if I had father or not. She never told me any story about him. Maybe he was dead or some-

---

27 - Jody William, Laureate 1997.

where with another woman. My mother was en-
gaged in sleeping with many men in order to feed our
home. In tears she said this was the beginning of my
pain. My mom was not only sleeping with many men
but she was a drug pusher that kept food on our table
and got her more drugs. Watching my mom was a
horrible scene of my childhood memories. By age
8 she began to literally sell me to a man in exchange
for money. What I experienced could not be put in
words.

My mother was privy to my ordeal." Lebeh shared
her story at age 17 with tears flowing down her cheek.
"In order to arrest the situation, my brother and I left
home and found shelter in this unfinished building.
Since I watched my mom do drugs and was involved
in transactional sex, I got involved in the trade to
support my brother and me. By age 19 I looked for
love through sex and found myself being used and
abused. In the process I got three precious children
from three different fathers. My fear was what would
happen to my children as I lived through my own ordeal."

Mothers are the first role models for a girl-child
therefore it is the responsibility of all mothers to
live exemplary lifestyles before your girl-child. At
Bridge of Hope we emphasize intentional mentoring
for girls, a process that exposes prominent women of
high moral value to girls through sharing their life
stories.

Another girl , whose name has been changed to
Watta in this book, shares her story: "My ordeal was
the fact that my parents were poor and we lived in a

dilapidated house far beyond the river in Sinkor 12th street community. My parents have no source of income so I got involved in the commercial sex trade and drugs. The results were that I eventually had unprotected sex and several abortions." With the prevalent high rate of HIV and AIDS or other STDS, Watta's life is at risk. In her tender age Watta's life should have been full of joy, but poverty and abandonment by her father robbed her of her joy. Life on the streets of Monrovia is tough without family support. Having listened to Watta's story, we encouraged her to always that the pains of her past should be the building blocks to push her to the place of rich fulfillment. Even though the past stays with you, I want to challenge you to always use it to make you a better person. My past is what makes me strong and wonderful. Let God write your story, wonderful and youthful Liberian girls. Do not allow your faults to frustrate your future.

Early and forced marriage . . .
tears and trauma of innocent girls

The practice of early marriage is a form of sexual violence against young girls and women. It is a practice that is common worldwide, especially in Africa South of the Sahara and South Asia. Liberia is no exception whereby young girls are often forced into marriage and into sexual school.[28] During the Liberian fourteen year civil war young girls and women were kidnapped and raped to be forcefully married.

---

28 - UN Department of Public Information, 1 United Nation Sec. Gen. Campaign: Unite to end violence against women. DPI/2546A, November 2009) pg.1

In some instances girls were offered to herbalists, witchdoctors, fetish shrines, traditional Zoes to provide full services including forced prostitution, domestic and sexual slaves.[29] Let God write your story captured some of the unimaginable stories from girls.

Mary Naplah (fictional name) was seated before an old brick house in the slum of Doe Community Monrovia, probably built by her grandparents and passed on to her late father, as she narrates her early and forced marriage ordeal with tears. "I was forcibly given to an older man age 40 as a wife at age fifteen. I spoke with Mary Naplah, age 50 from the Kru tribe (through a female interpreter.). Most of the texts were unedited thus remaining in the exact words of Mary to give the reader the true sense of her feelings. "I was taken from the Kru tribe in Liberia at an early age probably age 11 to Ghana by my parents. I was not told the reason for our travel to this strange country.

In Ghana I was introduced to an older man at age forty who was probably the age of my Father that he would be my husband. He was a seafarer who practically lived on the sea. I was terribly afraid to sleep in his room. He married many other wives and I was one of his wives but was the younger among them. He was never concerned about my education but my young and tender body. I never liked my so-called husband because he was forcing me to do things I did not want to" said Mary in her broken Liberian English. "I ran away from my family because I disliked

---

29 - http://www.lr.undp.org/UNDPwhatFightersSayLiberia_
Finalv3.pdf – Accessed April 14, 2012.

the man however, I gave him two fine boys. Mary is uneducated today at her old age but depends on her two boys and three girls to bring the joy she needs.

Early and forced marriage is when young girls are coerced to co-habitate at this early age. The aftermath is denial of basic rights to education, decisions, choices and the joy of a happy marriage. Marriage existing in all societies should be a formalized relationship with legal and/or social standing between individual men and women in which sexual relations are legitimized and as an arena for reproduction and child rearing that has state recognition.

Early marriage affects millions of children throughout the world, especially in Africa, the majority of whom are girls. They are forced to marry men they have never met before, and who are many years older than they are. Once married, they are responsible for looking after their husbands, the house, and the children they give birth to while still children themselves. They often have little knowledge about the responsibilities of being a wife and no information about sex education and childbirth.

These girls are forced to marry early for a number of reasons, including tradition, religion, and economics, and on sexual and reproductive health grounds.[30] The results of early marriage upon the girls can be severe. They are forced out of school without an education, their health is affected because their

_____

30 - Forum on Marriage and the Rights of Women and Girls. Early Marriage: Whose right to choose Carron Somerset, Wendy Agdagba. UK. Patersons Printers, UK. May 2000. Pg. 9-13.

bodies are too immature to give birth, they may become widows at a young age and they often must put up with domestic violence and sexual abuse.[31]

Throughout their lives they are discriminated against because they are girls, and early marriage is another act of discrimination and gender-related violence. This why *Let God Write Your Story* is capturing the tears and traumas of girls as means of creating awareness for government, society and community to take a proactive step towards this residential sexual abuse. Every child must be given the chance to live and experience her God-given purpose for life. At Bridge of Hope we seek to give every child the reason for her existence, thus creating a new identity for her (Jer. 29:11).

**Persistent gender violence
at the hands of the family members**

In our culture many children are sent from rural Liberia to the city to live with relatives for the sole purpose of education. Most of the time these children of the extended families end up being abused by these relations. Let God write your story capturing the tears and trauma of an innocent little girl that was brought to Monrovia from Lofa County to live her uncle. Krubo (fictional name) was just ten when she first arrived from Lofa County North of Liberia. The journey to the city for the first time was full of great excitement.

---

31 - Dr. David Okiror. James R. Davies Hospital, Joint Project of Government of Liberia and International Rescue Committee (IRC). Personal interview, June 6, 2011

A few years later her excitement turned into a nightmare. Krubo age 15, narrates her story: "My uncle was very abusive since my biological father died of unknown sickness and I have to be brought to Monrovia to live with him. I did not get good treatment from Uncle Akoi(fictional name). He beats on me most of the time when I make simple mistakes. At one time he attempted raping me but I fled from his presence and since that day he hated me the more. He called my biological father all kinds of names and made reference to him as a failure.

At one point he reminded me that because of my father's laziness, he died very poor. I could not withstand the abuse so I ran away from our home in Buzzi Quarter (Central Monrovia) and came to West Point. In West Point I met this man and even though he was far above my age, I married him. Today the both of us are partially living a happy life. My only regret is that my two girls are not in school like myself. What will become of us in the next Liberia?"

Young girls and women may be protected against the abuse of early marriage, by UN protocols but the reality in many African nations including post-conflict Liberia is that this nightmare is far from over. Young girls in particular are forced to become adults with the responsibilities of looking after their husbands, children and homes. It is very important for policy makers and their communities to recognize early marriage as a harmful traditional practice. For some girls early marriage is an escape from an abusive family, or is a result of a love match, but this applies only to a small percentage of those married.

Convention on the rights of the child argues that the views of a child be taken into account as well as the right to education; but many young girls in war-ravaged Liberia have been denied basic rights to education under the disguise of upholding tradition-al values such as early and forced marriage. Girls are married early because they are female and are expendable, the sooner they become someone else's responsibility. Early marriage contravenes inter-national and national human rights conventions; it deprives young girls of their right to an education, creating a vicious cycle of illiteracy, and early and fre-quent births. The key to preventing early marriage is providing transformational girls' education by rais-ing the awareness of parents, communities and policy makers about the negative impacts of early marriage on girls.

Parents and the community should be made aware of the rights of girls. Their contributions should be valued and they should not be seen as an economic burden or asset. The majority of mothers are fully aware of the implications of early marriage and are fearful for their daughters' futures, but they see no alternatives. Transformational girls' education seeks to empower girls and women by educating girls and their communities. It further seeks to raise aware-ness of good practice amongst NGOs and commu-nity groups, to teach them to listen to girls, involve them in planning and working with communities on changing cultures that have harmful practices.

Early marriage prevents girls from receiving edu-cation and can in turn prevent the children of young mothers from gaining an education.[32] Poverty and development in third world countries can't be adequately addressed until we recognize the need for the education of young girls. As Liberia transitions from war to peace, develops a stable economy and enhances the rule of law, it is vital that she targets gender equality as it relates to girls' education, and the need to ensure that girls get the same opportunities as boys to develop their potential and become full and equal members of society.

With an education, girls are given the chance to choose their own futures, not one chosen only by their parents or guardians. The issue of entry into and retention of the girl-child in the classroom for completion of the full educational cycle (KG through secondary) has been a major hurdle to achieving parity in the education of the girl child.[33]

Parents are encouraged to help their daughters stay at school. This is the focus of the sanitation, awareness and mobilization that this book is advocating, as evidenced in the case study of Bridge of Hope Girls' School.

---

32 - UNICEF Development Priority.1993.girls and women
33 - Policies to improve Girls' Education in Liberia. National Policy
    on Girls' Education. (Monrovia: Ministry of Education), 2005, 32.

Boys' Preference

There are traditional reasons people desire children. They are needed to remember their ancestors; without children there is no one to remember the ancestral spirits. Most Krahn children born in our culture are named after their dead parents. I am no exception to this as I was named after one dead auntie. The reason was never made known to me. All I used to hear is that I acted like her and her characteristics are seen in me.

Well, the dead live on in the people named after them. Without children, no one could offer drink offerings and sacrifices for the living dead, but in the face of their earnest desire to get children, they are selective.

In many cultures around the globe, there is no rejoicing when a girl-child is born. From her first breath, the girl-child's existence is tethered to cultural practices that at best, limit her potential and at worst, eliminate her life. For instance in India, the birth of a girl ushers in family worries concerning her future dowry. In Guatemala, girls at times seem to be valued primarily as workhorses, caring for younger siblings and toiling in the field—to the exclusion of their education. In Bangladesh, the potential of young girls is often eclipsed by early marriage, a practice that relieves parents of the "burden" of raising a girl. In China, newborn girls can die at the hands of parents who prefer a boy.

In Liberia, Guinea, Kenya and many other African countries, the painful process of female genital mutilation is routinely performed on some young girls to ensure their virginity.

In these places and many more, a son, not a daughter, is considered a blessing. Yet throughout his ministry, Jesus demonstrated a better way. Rejecting the assumptions of a patriarchal culture, Jesus boldly reached out to those considered "the lowest" of women as he reinforced their inherent worth as people equally loved and valued by an Almighty God. There is no room in Scripture for the favoring of boys over girls, no space for limiting the potential of girls simply because they are females.

The tears and traumas of a girl child are so real in our culture because of the emphasis parents placed on the boy child, most especially the father. Boy's preference has a visible profile and a difficult cultural issue we have to battle in our society. We have to deal with this because it is a negative cultural assumption most Africans have inherited from their forefathers. Liberia is no exception to this monster that has placed the girl child at a disadvantage. A girl-child is marginalized simply because she is a female.

> "Unlike apartheid and racism, gender prejudice is not acknowledged as a formally articulated behavioral precept or doctrine. But it clearly exists and has an impact on the female life-cycle."[34]

---

34 - Neera Kuckreja Sohoni. Consultant for UNICEF and other development agencies in India ffiliated Scholar at the Institute for Research on Women and Gender at Stanford University

Yah Gonseh, (fictional name) age 35, had given birth to five girls during her pre-arranged marriage. But when her girls were small, her husband decided to leave Yah because she had not produced a son.

He blamed her (I guess he didn't know a man's sperm determines the gender of a child) and he said she had shamed him by having only girls. He sold the family house, evicted his wife and daughters and gave them no money for food or school fees.

Then he married again and started a new family. He got two boys and another daughter out of the deal. Let God write her story and transform her life.

She is left helpless simply because she did not do what was not in her power to do. Yah was not depressed when she shared her sad history. She wore a colorful African dress and had a bright smile on her face as she told me how Jesus had been faithful to care for her after she was abandoned. "I had to learn to pray," she told me. "But today my girls are blessed and my oldest just finished her university education." Yah is fortunate.

Not all Liberian women have fared well after being abused, beaten, mutilated or abandoned. Up to 80 percent of women in Liberia have been sexually or physically abused, and the statistics are even higher in other African countries.

The story of my mother

In *Rewriting Your Story*, my first book, I captured the story of my biological mother. I am certain it fits well in this section of my third book. In my culture of origin, several things created a family reunion. One common event was death. In Liberia several tribes traditionally honor their dead kinsmen. The government even set aside the second Wednesday in March every year as Decoration Day—a day to remember and honor the dead kinsmen.[35] The Kwa speaking group (Krahn, Grebo, Kru, Bassa and Sarpo,) to which the researcher belongs, truly loved to honor their dead kinsmen. "Culturally, they believed like many Liberians that there exists a spirit world of their ancestors. When death occurs and the family is mourning, several things occur and many deep and hidden secrets are unearthed. It was time to hear deep cultural proverbs and history.

In the Krahn tribe, the section to which the researcher belongs, men and women who died in their very old age were considered not dead, but gone to join the home of their ancestors. Many legends about where they go and how they are received are told. Traditional and renowned singers, warriors, and mask dancers were invited to come and honor the dead. These kinds of cultural practices are deeply rooted in the lives of our kinsmen.

Some of these practices are good and have similarities with the Hebraic culture from which we draw lots of our Christian heritage. However, there are some aspects of our culture that are inherently cruel and inhumane.

---

35 - Fact Sheet No.23, Harmful Traditional Practices Affecting the Health of Women and Children. Convention on the Elimination of all forms of discrimination against women (art. 5 (a),adopted by General Assembly resolution 34/180 of 18 December 1979.

For example, there is nothing wrong with the wife mourning her dead husband, but something is certainly wrong for the community to forcibly ask the widow to get married to the surviving brother or uncle simply because she is considered 'property' bought by the family.[36]

It is cruel and barbaric to demoralize the woman by allowing her to sleep alone with the corpse of her dead husband for the first three days. It is against her right to refuse her a meal or shower and make mockery of her while she is grieving her late husband. It is wrong and evil to deny the woman every property she and her late husband had acquired simply in the name of not bearing a child-- most especially a boy child for the deceased husband. This was just the tip of the iceberg of the culture into which the researcher was born.

When my oldest sister, Sophia,(pseudonym) died on July 20, 2008 in a tragic motor accident, there were strange revelations about our late mother. Stephen Wesseh (pseudonym) said "one day a cruel tax collector came from Monrovia (along the coast, the home of the freed black slaves from America) to our rural village in Northern Liberia to collect hut taxes."[37]

According to the story, one particular family did not have the amount charged for the hut tax. The consequence was that the head of the family was

---

36 - Chief Kpadeh Flomo. (pseudonym) Oral History of Krahn tradition. Personal Interview Oct. 6, 2014
37 - Hut tax System in Liberia Narrated (Cited) Rewriting Your Story. Retrieved from: https://archives.columbusstate.edu/gah/1996/41-60.

caught, tied, and with his face lifted up was placed under a blazing sun for failure to pay the hut tax. In this specific case, the prisoner was my maternal grand-uncle. My grand-uncle, who was the head of the family, took my late mother and pawned her to my late father Peter Weka Geesanhun (pseudonym) as a guarantor until the amount in question was refunded. Accordingly, it was difficult to retrieve the money and my mother remained a pawn and became the youngest wife of my father. This was a form of neo-slavery among the tribes.[38] It is very essential to understand the implication of the "Pawn System." This was the practice of chiefs of certain tribes sending children of their tribe to coastal tribes for work for payment to the chief. History tells us that the situation between the African natives and successive governments headed by the settlers from America got much worse. Inhumane practices went beyond unfair taxation as the government went to the greatest extremes of dehumanization–they started selling inhabitants from the interior regions into slavery for even more cash.[39]

My mother went into a home, which already had several other wives and became the youngest in the midst of these older women. She was loved and cherished according to the story, probably because of her tender age and beauty. Accordingly, my mother died under mysterious circumstances. Whatever the ac-

---

38 - Researcher. Rewriting Your Story Oral story of tax collectors and slavery in the Krahn culture. Retrieved from: https://archives.columbusstate.edu/gah/1996/41-60.
39 - Ibid.

tual history was, I grew up as a partial orphan and indigent child. Today my love for orphans, disadvantaged and indigent children has deepened simply because I tasted what it meant to be impoverished and live in an illiterate society. As a boy growing up in the village, my life was restricted to the happenings around me. Boys were growing up to become fathers at an early age without formal education, while girls were becoming ill-prepared mothers. Young girls and boys were forced into *Sande'* and *Poro* societies (Bush schools) as a means of passage to adulthood.[40]

My dad attempted once to educate my sisters but the result was unfortunate as several of them got sexually exploited by young boys and some were impregnated by the village teachers. My dad in turn shut the doors on the rest of the sisters and they were given into early marriages after their initial rites. "Education alone is obviously not enough to solve the world's problems, but it remains an essential factor in any development activity."[41]

Interestingly my wife, Victoria, narrated her own story in an interview: "I had a similar background where my mother, at a tender age and without formal education, was forced into early marriage to a seafarer with several other wives. My mother was not loved. Hence, me and the rest of my siblings suffered rejection and discrimination and did not experience

40 - Sande' and Poro societies (Bush Schools) Retrieved from: http://www.everyculture.com/Ja-Ma/Liberia.html#ixzz34P3Kqmkw
41 - Researcher. Rewriting Your Story. Transforming your story into glory. Nairobi. 2013.
42 - Co-Founder, Central New Matadi. Personal Interview. May 25, 2015.

the love of a real father."[42] God brought us together twenty three years ago and gave us the same deep passion for the plight of girls in our community after studies at the Nairobi Evangelical Graduate School of Theology in 2004. "Fortified with the convictions about girls thriving in certain educational settings, prime among the qualities of which are academic, innovative, girl-valuing girls' school, safe-space, we set out to establish a single-sex school that met our expectations."[43] God honored our expectations and brought students from diverse socio-economic backgrounds into Bridge of Hope Girls' School. *Let God Write Your Story* captures the stories of their transformation . . .

"My name is Melisia Karlay (pseudonym), age 17, grade 6; I took my primary school examinations in the 2010/2011 academic school year. My education had previously been cut off because of the last part of the war in 2003. When I came with my family to Central New Matadi Slum community, it was difficult for me to attend the regular school because I was 12 years old and far older than most girls in my class. I am happy that my uncle told me about a special school in our community for girls like me. I was glad to be a student at Bridge of Hope Girls' School Accelerated Learning Program (ALP). I was 19 years old when I sat for my first public examinations at the Bridge of Hope Girls' School." When asked how she felt about the exams, her usual hard facial expression became softened and, using both hands, she gave a double thumb-up gesture and said "It was fine". Melisia is optimistic that she will make it through and she looks forward to enrolling in high school in the next academic year. "When I finish my education, I want to become a lawyer," she concluded."[44]

My name is Esther Yeanay (pseudonym), a 7th grade student at BOH. I was born to a drug-addicted father who was unable to properly care for me and my siblings. At an early age of 5 years old, we were taken to the orphanage home and we remained there until I was 16. During those eleven years, the school at the orphanage was in a very poor condition and learning was unstable. Three years ago my uncle brought me to this new school (BOH) where there are all girls and our learning has never been disrupted; even though I missed my male friends in my former school. [45]

Stories of explicit transformation

Jamestta Flomo (pseudonym), age 16, grade 3. I came to the Matadi community two years ago from West Point (one of the slums communities) to live with my nephew and his wife. My learning has delayed because my parents could not afford to pay my

---

44 - Melisia Karlay (pseudonym) Grade 7 Student. BOH. Personal Interview . June 20, 2015.
45 - Esther Yeanay (pseudonym) 7th grade student. BOH. Personal Interview. June 20, 2015.

school fees. I am 16 and just starting grade 3. I feel ashamed but I am hoping since this is an all-girls school my female friends would help me learn faster.

"My name is Mary Togba (pseudonym),[46] 14; I hail from the Kpelle tribe in Central Liberia. I have never been to any school. This year I was brought to BOH to form part of the kindergarten class. I know I am older than most of the girls in my class. I do not write or speak English well. I had just graduated [referring to the traditional bush school] and I was forcibly taken to town by my elder sister who is a third year college student. In spite of my age, I was accepted at BOH and brought to this special program (ALP -Accelerated Learning program).[47]

The story of (Valare Koon pseudonym), 16: "I am a student of BOH, and I live in the Lakpazee slum community. I entered BOH five years ago as a first grade student. It was difficult for me to accept this class; because I was older than all the girls. I was feeling ashamed to sit in the class with these younger girls. I felt completely different in their midst because of my age and the fact that I could not speak and write well. My parents had refused for me to come to the city to attend, even though we had no school in our village. Another thing about my village was that girls were forced to go to the bush school. My older sister

---

46 - (Pseudonym)
47 - NRC/ALP. Retired from; http://www.nrc.no/ (ALP which cater to specific learning conditions like that of Mary and Princess). The Accelerated Learning Program targets over-aged children (10 to 17 years), who dropped out of school or never went to school because of the war, and allows these children to complete the six years of primary school in three academic years.

had to convince my mother to bring me to Monrovia for school. Thank God that today I am a 7th grade student and can read and write well.

My only concern has to do with my sisters that are growing up in the village without school; I am afraid that they might go to the bush school and after that get married soon.[48]

I want to share the words of J. Lee Grady of Charisma: "My dream is that the church—not only in Africa but throughout the world—will stop playing in the shallow waters of feel-good, me-centered Christianity and decide to apply the gospel of Christ to the injustices of the world."[49]

My heart's desire for Africa is that leaders of the Church will start applying the gospel to the daily injustices and discriminations meted against innocent girls and women in our community in the name of boys' preference.

---

48 - Valare Koon (pseudonym). 8th grade student. BOH. Personal Interview. Matadi, October 12, 2014.
49 - J. Lee Grady is *contributing editor* of Charisma.

LET

God

WRITE YOUR STORY

Chapter 4

Creating New Identity

FOR LIBERIAN GIRLS

Many innocent girls and women living in Liberia before and after the civil war have faced numerous challenges, rooted in traditions, influenced by poverty and executed as oppression. As a result, uneducated, impoverished and exploited girls face a life without hope.

The Bridge of Hope Girls' School is one of the many institutions established and dedicated to breaking the cycle of despair that often is handed down in Liberia from one generation of women to the next. As Bridge of Hope follows Jesus' call to bring hope to marginalized people, girls and women are linked to resources, services and opportunities for physical, mental, emotional and spiritual development.

Trash is turning into treasures and oppression into empowerment for the girl children whose lives Bridge of Hope is able to touch. It is our prayer that we will continue to be relevant tools in the hands of the Lord to transform the lives of these disadvantaged girls. We exist to enhance life and sustain hope in these precious girls who lives have been devalued by themselves or the community.

Stories of transformation

"For me I started this school from 3rd grade second period where I was looked down upon by other students that said I will not make it. But God helped me to make it and now I am in the 8th grade and I am still here and God is still helping me. I thank him. I love this school a lot because of the discipline they take us through... helping us to learn not only for today but for the future. I pray for God to help the school with money so as for me to continue my 12th grade education here. I know he will do so because He is the God of everything."

Why would Bridge of Hope Girls' School focus on the girl child in a nation where both boys and girls have been impoverished by high degree of illiteracy? The words of Robert A. Seiple, former World Vision President clearly conveyed the objectives:

> "There is a rent in the fabric of our humanity. Because in our increasingly dysfunctional world that continues to work against those most marginalized, there is a rent in the fabric of young lives, and the vulnerability of little girls is most exposed."[50]

I would also like to borrow from Mark Twain, in language that is as profound as it is humorous:

"What, sir, would the people of the earth be without women? They be scare, almighty scare."[51]

---

50 - Robert A. Seiple. In the Garment a Rent.
The 1998 Washington Forum Perspectives on Our Global Future. www. worldvision.org © 1998 World Vision Inc.
51 - Ibid.

The vision and educational philosophy of the founding fathers and mothers of Bridge of Hope Girls' School is not a segregated look at girls' or women's issues. What is at stake regarding the girl-child should be relevant and of concern to anyone who has ever had a sister, a daughter or a mother—and that is everybody.

Taking care of little girls is not just women's responsibility. In fact, we in faith-based communities need to cultivate men who are willing to incarnate Jesus' tenderness toward children in general, and toward women and girls in particular. What Jesus Christ demands from all of us is caring for the "least of these."

Transforming stories of girls and their mothers

Let God Write Your Story is not only the story of girls at BOH, but we also reached the mothers of these girls. As we implemented the Water with Blessing project in slum communities, we asked the women to share some of the challenges they are facing with men in their community. So many of them struggled with so much fear, but here are some of the responses they shared with us. One mother shared with us "we are beaten by our husbands, and then we are told never to report the abuse to authorities.

We are denied basic education–our husbands will send the boys to school while the girls are told to stay at home, fetch water and cook." The stories were endless: "We are expected to be quiet and obedient, and we must kneel in the presence of men. Many of our husbands live in adultery, or they marry second, third, or fourth wives and bring all the children into our homes."

As Let God Write Your Story captured the tears and traumas of teenage girls and women, they were more open to us and shared more stories: "We are expected to produce many children, but we do not have the money to take care of them—and sometimes our husbands abandon us. We have been raped and sexually abused, so we feel inferior.   Boys are favored over girls, so we have low self-esteem.

It was so sad that even in the Church, the place of hope, did not offer help for these hopeless women:·"When we see only male leaders in the church, we wonder if there is a place for us there. Some men manipulate the Word of God to tell us that it is right of only men to lead in the church. We are under compulsion to submit to abuse and adultery."

Chapter 5

Cultivating Safe Space

FOR LIBERIAN GIRLS

Creating a safe-space for girls should be a deliberate decision on the part of everyone including church leaders, community leaders, and policy makers in our society that is man's dominated and yet torn apart by high rate of illiteracy. It begins with realizing the enormous benefits of educating a girl-child. The benefits of educating girls have a long impact on the countries, families, and the girls themselves. This initiative is so substantial that some economists, including Lawrence Summers, a former Harvard University president and former director of President Obama's National Economic Council, have stated that "educating girls may be the single highest return investment in the developing world."[52] In addition, educating girls not only stimulates economic growth, it improves the well-being of women and gives them more agencies in their communities and countries.[53]

---

52 - Lawrence H. Summers. 1994. "Investing in All the People: Educating Women in Developing Countries." EDI Seminar Paper No. 45. Washington, D.C.: World Bank.
53 - Barbara Herz and Gene B. Sperling. 2004. "What Works in Girls' Education: Evidence and Policies from the Developing World." Washington, D.C.: Council on Foreign Relations.

Testimonies of Parents at PTA Meeting

"My daughter came to BOH when she was 8. During her kindergarten graduation an instructor from BOH recognized her performance and encouraged me to enroll her at BOH. We did not have the fees necessary for registration at BOH, so the instructor helped her to enroll in 2008. Grace (pseudoymn), the youngest of our five children, lives with us in Matadi, a suburb of Monrovia, about ten minutes from the school.

During the rainy season, travel to the school is difficult because of the swamps that surround our home. Both of us are unemployed . . . her mother does petty trading at the local market, while at times I find day hire. BOH Girls' School is vital for girls like my daughter, who might not be in school without such an institution. Illiteracy continues to be very high in our culture where education for girls and women is traditionally and culturally discouraged, and many of our girls are given in early and forced marriages. My daughter is in the 7th grade and is able to read well, and can work independently.

What excites me the most is that my daughter's behaviors have immensely improved; less contacts with boys and is focused."[54]

"Our daughter Fasko Washington (pseudonym) was never interested in attending church with us four years ago until she enrolled at the Bridge of Hope Girls School. We are members of the Living Way

---

54 - Moses Gbarglo (pseudonym) Parent. Personal Interview. Central New Matadi Community. October 2015.

Baptist Church and currently Fasko is very active in her Sunday school classes and even leading family devotions at home. Our daughter's attitude towards us and her siblings has changed including her approach to household chores. In my mind, changes and learning have taken place in the past five years of enrollment at this school. Our big challenge is where do we take her after completion at BOH?"[55]

At Bridge of Hope our goal is to create a new identity for Liberian girls. It starts with giving them quality Christian education at the primary level and junior high level in line with the universal primary education (UPE), which is one of the United Nations Development Goals, along with gender equality. Educating greater numbers of women and girls also helps meet the growing need for teachers and health workers, which is crucial for post conflict Liberia in which women and girls must be served by women teachers and doctors.

In the words of Nobel Laureate Amartya Sen, "when women are educated they gain voice and agency in their lives (safe-space) giving them more economic opportunities, encouraging women's political participation, and transforming society for the better. These benefits begin sooner than may appear at first glance.[56] Keeping girls in school through 10th-12th grade quickly produces positive changes. These girls do not marry young; they can cope better in the 21st

---

55 - Tendee Washington (pseudonym). Parent. Personal Interview. Fiamah Community . October 27, 2015.
56 - Amartya Sen. 2000. Development as Freedom. New York: Anchor Books.

century, help their families, and take better advantage of new opportunities as economic and social circumstances change. The well-being of the girl-child is our ultimate concern at Bridge of Hope. It is very clear from research that educating girls is the surest path to smaller, healthier families.

Women spend more time than men do in caring for children. Studies find that resources that women control go more directly to help the family than do the resources that men control. The more education a woman has, the more likely it is she can earn a higher income, which will go to benefit her family. In addition, when women are educated they and their husbands tend to want smaller families and to invest more in the health and education of each child.

In countries where three-fourths of women have a secondary education, women typically have two or three children, the children are more likely to attend school and child mortality drops as family income rises. [57]

According to many studies, a year of schooling for the mother beyond the average in her country cuts infant mortality by 5 percent to 10 percent. [58]   Where mothers are educated, girls and boys generally go to school longer and study more. Often the mother's education matters more than the father's, especially in countries where the gap in schooling between girls

---

57 - Herz and Sperling 2004.
58 - T. Paul Schultz. 1993. "Returns to Women's Schooling."
In Elizabeth King and M. Anne Hill, eds., *Women's Education in Developing Countries: Barriers, Benefits, and Policy.* Baltimore: Johns Hopkins University Press.

and boys is greatest.[59] We have the ability to mend
the rent in the garment. We have the ability, through
God our Savior, to provide a holistic covering, a covering of protection—of spiritual, physical and emotional protection for little girls of every nation.

Let God Write Your Story is an encouragement to
all to take care of these girls. Be especially sensitive
to all who are overlooked. Take care of the special
needs of one of the least of these—the girl-child, and
as you do so, you will be a sign and a witness to the
very kingdom of God.

Family Transforming Testimony

When Victoria and I got married two and half decades ago she was a high school graduate and had a
desire to further her education but had some deep
family complexities. We agreed to educate her beyond high school. In 1998 when I became the first
President at the Liberia Christian College (A Christian education arm of the African Christians Fellowship International ACFI), she sat the placement
exams and after a successful passing, she enrolled as
one of the first students. After four years she graduated with a bachelor of arts degree in business administration. She has been a source of inspiration and real
support for the education of our three girls.

---

59 - Deon Filmer. 2000. "The Structure of Social Disparities
in Education: Gender and Wealth." Policy Research Working
Paper No. 2268, World Bank Development Research Group/
Poverty Reduction and Economic Management Network.
Washington, D.C.: World Bank. And: Jere Behrman, et al.
1999. "Women's Schooling, Home Teaching, and Economic
Growth." *Journal of Political Economy*.

At present, our first daughter Jackie has also earned a bachelor's degree in Business Management with specific emphasis on Health Management.

Pauline earned a bachelor's degree in biology from one of the prestigious universities in Liberia (Cuttington University College) and now a fourth year student at the AM Doglitti College of Medicine aspiring to be a medical doctor (pediatrician). Peace, the last of our daughters, is a graduating senior at the Cuttington University College aspiring to be an accountant.

Girls who are literate, and particularly girls who reach secondary school, are more likely to avoid HIV/AIDS because they can better obtain information, stand up for themselves and take more control of their lives.[60] They will in turn have smaller, healthier and better educated families that will help raise economic productivity, equip people to enter new lines of work, ease environmental pressures and slow population growth, which many countries consider important changes.[61]

---

60 - Herz and Sperling 2004; Mead Over. 1998. "The Effects of Societal Variables on Urban Rates of HIV Infection in Developing Countries: An Exploratory Analysis." In Martha Ainsworth, Lieve Fransen, and Mead Over, eds, *Confronting AIDS: Evidence from the Developing World*. Brussels and Washington, D.C.: European Commission and World Bank; UNESCO 2002c. "Press Release for A Strategic Approach: HIV/AIDS and Education." Available at http://portal.unesco.org/ev.php?URL. And: Damien De Walque. 2004. "How Does Educational Attainment Affect the Risk of Being Infected by HIV/AIDS? Evidence from a General Population Cohort in Rural Uganda." World Bank Development Research Group Working Paper. Washington, D.C.: World Bank. March.
61 - Herz and Sperling 2004.

Testimony of Girls' transformation

"My name is Wenneta Paye (pseudonym), age 17, 2008/2009 graduate of the BOH. Presently I am in the 12th grade at the Faith International School. "I am proud to be an alumnus of BOH." It is my desire after my high school education to enter the University of Liberia. I have chosen law as my future career. I am confident I will make it to the University after my graduation because of my preparations at my former school.

Even though it was difficult and restricted us to limit our contact with boys, I am glad that I was able to withstand all of the tough discipline. I am grateful to the administration of BOH for all they have done for me to enable me to be in the 12th grade. I have had no problem in my new school especially with my lessons, discipline, obeying authority, and remaining focused. I am glad I am not pregnant and not willing to trade my body for grades in this new school." The Principal alluded to this transformation when she asserted: "The success of alumni one year after graduation is directly the result of the learning experiences at BOH; evidenced by the conducive learning environment; girl friendly curriculum and role model instructors to the girls."

Let God Write Your Story realized that the education philosophy of Bridge of Hope was responsible for the success stories of the girls after graduation: "The success which alumni experienced after graduation is the result of a collaborative effort by the school and the girls themselves in direct support of the vision of creating a new identity for Liberian girls and empowering the next generation. In the past eight years, we have had six graduations and award programs with over 200 students graduating from the primary division to secondary levels. Our present records show that 75% of our girls are still progressing towards completing secondary school while 25% are anticipating entering universities.

The story of the Christian education model captured in this book is an alternative to girls' education in post conflict Liberia and is in consonance with the education philosophy of Liberia, which is to guide the provision of education for all Liberians so that they are able to pursue knowledge and skills, manifest excellence in performance and moral uprightness, defend democratic ideals, and accept and value other persons on the basis of their personal worth and dignity, irrespective of gender, religion, ethnic, origin, or any other discriminatory characteristics.

Conclusion

As we have journeyed through pieces of literature, it has revealed the slow growth and development of girls' education in post-conflict Liberia, evidenced by the cultural and religious response to girls' education which has a visible profile of a limited number of girls' schools throughout the nation. This limitation has resulted in an unbalanced ratio or huge disparity between boys to girls in education.

Let God Write Your Story has also unveiled some hindrances to girl-child education and advancement. Traditional cultural beliefs and practices, such as initiation rites, early and forced marriages, boys' preference, child labor or prostitution are consistent hurdles placed in the pathway of girl-child seeking education and advancement. However, as we journey through this captivating story of a transformational Christian education model at Bridge of Hope, I hope it has given you a renewed passion to develop a balanced perspective for a girl-child in your community.

Let God Write Your Story has captured the transformed social narratives of disadvantaged girls in the informal setting of Matadi, Monrovia. I pray that as you read through these stories of explicit transformation, your own life has been transformed and you are ready to join us as we 'champion this cause' for these marginalized girls.

This new paradigm, when embraced, can minimize high cultural disparity between boys and girls in education, increase entry and retention, progression and completion of girls as well as help the girl-child discover meaning in life, promote self-confidence and self-esteem. It is a glaring fact that women are vital in the education and eventual socialization of their child. Hence when we educate a girl-child we are educating a nation and shutting the door to poverty, disease, harmful traditional practices and high rate of illiteracy. In conclusion, in this passionate appeal for educating the girl-child in post-conflict Liberia, we deeply treasured the precious words of the former UN Secretary Kofi Annan "Knowledge is power. Information is liberating. Education is the premise of progress, in every society, in every family." This concept has been one of the driving forces in championing the cause of girls' education in post war Liberia.

Join the Girls

As together they sing the
"school ode" during morning devotions:

We are the girls of Liberia
Trusting in the Lord

Our tears have been turned into victory . . .
for you; we are strong and lifted by the Lord.

Bridge of Hope Girls' School we love you,
Bridge of Hope Girls' School we honor you . . .
to you we will always be true.

We will ever hail thee . . .
Bridge of Hope Girls' School.

Sis. Marilyn Rossiter
Co-Founder / BOH

LET

God

WRITE YOUR STORY

About the Author

Bishop Dr. Jackson G. Weah is a 1988 graduate of the African Bible College University (Cum laude') with BA in Biblical Studies and Minor in Christian Education. He also earned a Master of Arts Degree in Historical Studies - June 2004 from the Nairobi Evangelical Graduate School of Theology (NEGST) now Africa International University (AIU) in Nairobi Kenya.

In July 2017 he earned a Degree of Doctor of Ministry from the Africa International (AIU). Emphasis on "Transformational Leadership and Conflict Transformation."

Ministry Experience

Bishop Dr. Weah is a Senior Pastor and General Overseer of the Hope Renewal Ministries International (Hope of Praise Church) located in Central New Matadi Monrovia Liberia, a church he and his wife Pastor/Mot. Victoria G. Weah pioneered in 2004 after his studies in Kenya. Hope of Praise was established on Feb. 4, 2006 and has a membership of over three hundred. It has over ten churches across Liberia. Bishop Dr. Weah is also the Founder of Bridge of Hope Girls' School that caters to disadvantaged girls in post war Liberia. This school is creating new identities for Liberian girls and empowering the next generation.

By calling Bishop Dr. Weah is a preacher–teacher. Known in Liberia as a trainer of grass root church leaders and pastors and conference speaker. He has a deep passion for indigenous African Christianity.

Academic and Administrative Experiences:

He has served as President of the Liberia Christian College, Professor and Academic Dean at seminaries in Liberia including Bryant Theological Seminary, Liberty Theological Seminary and Monrovia Bible College. Bishop Dr. Weah is currently an Adjunct Professors at Cuttington University Graduate School and AME University Graduate School, and Bradley Browne Liberia Baptist Theological Seminary Graduate School respectively.

He currently serves as the National Bishop of the Kingdom Covenant Ministries International (KCMI). A Fellowship of over three hundred churches in Liberia that trains rural pastors and church leaders. Bishop Dr. Weah is also the Regional Bishop of the Tabernacle of Praise Association of Churches a West Africa Diocese that include (Liberia, Guinea, Burkina Faso, and Ghana). .

He has traveled, preached and taught widely in West and East Africa as well as in the United States and Israel.He is also the author of "Rewriting Your Story" – Strength to transform your story into glory. Bishop Dr. Weah recently authored his second book *"Yesterday Character of God"*–Fanning hope in the flames of fire. His passion for ministry is –"Renewing the hope of nation in integrity and holiness." He is happily married to Pastor/Mot. Victoria G. Weah, Resident Pastor of the Hope of Praise Church and the union is blessed with three precious girls (Patience, Pauline and Peace) and two wonderful grandchildren (Shelby and Lawrett).

Bridge of Hope